Blossom the Butterfly!

Shawnitha Cooper

ISBN 979-8-88616-602-6 (paperback)
ISBN 979-8-88616-603-3 (digital)

Christian Faith Publishing
832 Park Avenue
Meadville, PA 16335
www.christianfaithpublishing.com

Printed in the United States of America

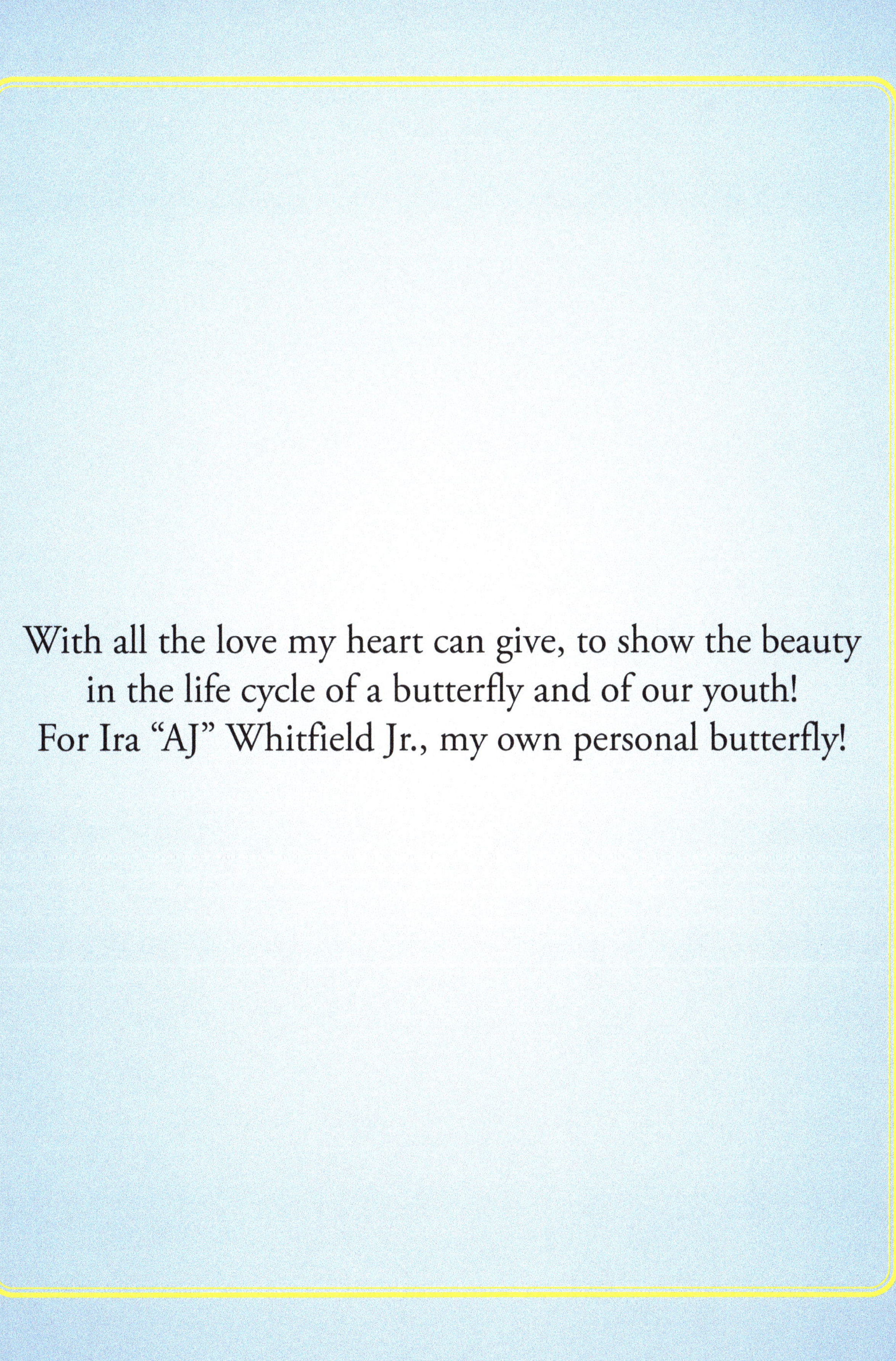

With all the love my heart can give, to show the beauty
in the life cycle of a butterfly and of our youth!
For Ira "AJ" Whitfield Jr., my own personal butterfly!

On one beautiful summer day,
Up in a tree far away,
Resting on a leaf so nice and calm
Was a little round egg, small and young.

Inside, what could it be?
A bird, a beetle, or a bee?
Inside was something beautiful,
A little caterpillar that would come to be.

Blossom was her name,
And she was very shy.
While stuck in her shell,
She didn't know why.

What would the world be like? she wondered,
Tucked and hidden away from everyone and
    everything.
Blossom wasn't sure what her feelings really meant,
Eager to explore the outside world and make new
    friends.

Blossom wasn't quite sure where she would begin.

Then one beautiful day, something miraculous started
    to take place.
Blossom's shell began to hatch.
As the sunlight crept through, she wasn't sure what
    to do.

While all eyes waited for her to emerge,
Blossom couldn't find the confidence to show herself.
Afraid of what the others might think,
Blossom tucked herself away and continued to shrink.

Then out of the shadows
A friendly voice from Ollie the Owl said to her,
"Oh, Blossom. Oh, Blossom, my dear.
Come out and draw near!"

Slowly peeking through the cracks,
She felt she just wasn't quite ready yet.
"Oh, no!" Blossom screeched.
"I have no wings, no pretty colors or anything."

"Be patient, my dear.
Your beauty will come within the year," said Ollie.
Feeling nervous and afraid, she just wanted to hide
   away,
Afraid of the whispers and stares from her peers.

Blossom trembled in fear.

Again, Ollie called out to her,
"Oh, Blossom, my dear, be confident and believe in
    yourself.
You can do it and draw near."

Slowly crawling out of the mist,
Blossom couldn't believe all the beauty she saw could
    be so bliss.
Happy and excited to see all the bright colors!
She finally felt ready to meet the others.

As she slowly crawled near,
She noticed that all others were full of feathers and furs,
Of every shape and size.
Even some had bright colors that matched one another.

Oh, no! Blossom thought.
Everyone will see that I'm different.
I'm small with no fur or feathers,
No bright color or any wings. I don't have anything.

Stopped in her tracks,
She wanted to turn back.
Wishing she could wait until she had fully bloomed,
Blossom thought because she was different her
    friendships would be doomed.

Seeing her fear, Ollie said to her,
"Blossom, it's okay to be different.
We were all made with unique features,
To one day become beautiful creatures."

They began to laugh and snicker.
"What is she? What is she?"
They began to buzz—
The bees, the squirrels, the birds, and the moles.

"What is she?" No one knew.
Blossom replied in a voice so strong,
"I will become a butterfly. Just wait and see.
Go ahead if you must and laugh at me."

Blossom and Ollie enjoyed their days
Casting all cares away.
Not having a care in the world,
Blossom just tried to stay focused on growing to be
    a beautiful and courageous girl.

One day, after a nice lunch of bunches of leaves,
Blossom started to feel more at ease.
As her tummy began to grow full of pleasure,
She knew the leaves would help her grow better.

Munching and snacking the entire day,
She began to notice her skin shedding away.

"Oh, no!" Blossom screeched.
"Everyone, please turn and look away from me!"

Blossom had no idea what was happening,
Only that her skin was casting.
Not aware this was part of her growth,
She just wanted to keep it hidden so that the others
    wouldn't know.

She felt ashamed and wanted to hide.

Her dear friend Ollie noticed and pulled her aside.
"Oh, Blossom, my dear, no need to be ashamed.
We all grow a few sizes—it's part of growth and change!"

Ollie's words were comforting to Blossom,
So she continued on chomping.
After a few days of munching and snacking,
She suddenly beheld the pounds she was packing.

Blossom had feasted until she was nice and full.
Her last layer rolled right off without a pull.
Now delighted and well pleased,
She decided it was time to sit and enjoy the breeze.

Resting her feet and her jaws,
She was glad that she decided to take a pause.

Blossom worried if she hurt her tummy from all the
    feasting.
She felt the others might poke fun if they knew what
    she was thinking.

Not wanting the others to know how she felt,
She began to climb to the treetop, to wrap herself
    like a quilt.
She just wanted to hide away,
Not carrying what anyone had to say.

Ollie pleaded and begged for her to stay,
But Blossom just wanted to go and tuck away.
"Blossom, my dear, don't worry about what others
    think.
You were made good enough and loved no matter
    what," Ollie said to his dear friend.

Blossom continued to climb higher and higher.
Up high in the tree, she began wrapping her head,
    chest, arms, and legs.
Covered and tucked from head to toe,
To sleep was the only thing she wanted to do.

Exhausted at last, she fell asleep in her cast.
Monday, Tuesday, Wednesday had passed.
Not a peep from Blossom.
Not a sound from her cast.

Thursday, Friday, Saturday had gone by.
Still there was nothing, not the smallest wave "Hi."
Ollie began to worry as the week flew by.
Not one squeak or a gentle voice "Hi."

Ollie remembered not to worry or be upset.
It wasn't time for his friend to come out yet.
Then late one afternoon,
Blossom made a spectacular cocoon.

Small, hard, and closed well.
Things were taking place inside.
Ollie knew very well.
The others figured it was magic, nothing much to
    hide.

Ollie proclaimed,
"She's a lot different from you and me.
We must give her rest.
That way she will come out her best."

At the end of the week,
Everyone heard a squeak.
The cocoon was cracking.
Something was starting to happen.

Blossom opened her big blue eyes,
Forgetting the sad days that had come to pass,
Of constantly feeling ashamed
And worried if everyone would laugh.

Blossom stretched and wiggled to get set free.
Something felt stuck, and she thought it was her knee.
She kicked some more until her cocoon cracked.
She stretched her neck out and noticed something
    on her back.

"What are those?" Blossom asked.
"I never had these upon my back."

Stretching out just a little bit more, she was finally
    free.
Blossom turned to see what the new things upon her
    back could be.

All the others were shocked and amazed!
"What are the things upon her back?" everyone
    started to ask.
Ollie answered, "Those are not things.
Blossom has grown her beautiful wings!"

Blossom looked out over the land afar,
Wondering what lay beyond the road of black tar.

As she looked back to say goodbye,
She knew it was time to spread her wings and fly.

Feeling courageous and confident as ever,
She knew the world was before her to be one great
    adventure.
The world was now her new home.
She was ready to start her new journey on her own.

Blossom's heart filled with joy
Remembering her dear friend Ollie's voice,
Telling her to be confident and never ashamed.
Everyone is made different and goes through their
    own growth changes.

Blossom knew that trusting the life cycle
Gave her the courage to endure life changes.
Blossom had become what she always intended to be.
A butterfly! Unique and free!

Author Message

Always remember no matter what the world throws your way, God loves you and made you unique in his image, just like Blossom. You will change and grow to be courageous and victorious as promised in his Word. You will transform into someone unique and strong. Therefore, remember not to grow weary in doing things right. Trust the process. Whenever the world makes you feel unwanted or ashamed, always remember whose you are and what our Lord above proclaimed: "You are fearfully and wonderfully made" (Psalm 139:14).

About the Author

Shawnitha "Shawn" Cooper is the founder of Susta's IN Unity, a nonprofit organization focusing on the development and spiritual growth of women in the community to help them lead and connect in society. With a BA in speech communications, MA in media communications, and MA in management and leadership, she has held multiple positions in leadership, managing and training others to succeed in their careers.

Born in September 1983 to a single mother and being the first grandchild, she learned very early how important it was to be kind to others, to be strong, and to always lend a helping hand when needed. While growing in her faith, it makes it easy for her to uplift and be a shoulder to those around her. Now that she finally feels that she is following the purpose set forth for her, she prays that she continues to help others be inspired to live a fulfilled life by helping them find and succeed in their purpose through her faith.